GIRL YOU **CAN** WIN!

PRAISES FOR *GIRL, YOU CAN WIN!*

"One of the best devotionals I've read in a while. I love how the writer captured the audience with scripture and used the most edifying scriptures to describe each chapter and made me feel like "Girl, I got this, I really can win!""

-DeJ'a Lowery- President of Single Ministries (Faith Clinic Church of God in Christ)

"While reading, I realized I was able to refer to this devotional for every season of my life. Girl, You Can Win! is not only a devotional, but it's a learning experience. Being immersed in encouragement and the teachings of Christ, makes it much easier to remember God's promises and get me through those gloomy days that life brings. Thank you!"

- Karen Belle, LLBSW

Girl, You Can Win! meets every woman where she is, without judgement. Get this book.

- *Missionary Regina Williams*

"I highly recommend "Girl, You Can Win!" to women of all ages. Reading this devotional will leave you inspired and ready to face whatever challenges life may bring. I consider it a must have and a must read. Afterwards, I promise, you will know YOU CAN WIN!"

– Angel Brock, President of Young Women With Purpose

"Girl You Can Win! is intentional; I believe that every woman who reads it would feel as though it is written specifically for them. It brings unspoken issues to the forefront of the mind and challenges the reader to put forth action to change for the better, enabling them to win!"

–Missionary Illicisa Jones

Authoress Tiara Moore has done it again. "Girl, You Can Win!" is skillfully written and full of the substance one looks for in a devotional. Led by the spirit of the Lord, Moore delivers an easy, yet impactful read. Perfect for any young Christian woman's arsenal.

–Julie Flowers

Publisher
Girl You Can Win
Copyright @2020 by Tiara Moore

Library of Congress Cataloging Data
Girl You Can Win / Tiara Moore
ISBN: 979-864-388-8994

All rights reserved. No part of this book may be reproduced in any form on by an electronic or mechanical means, including information storage and retrieval systems, without permission in writing from the publisher, except by a reviewer who may quote brief passages in a review.

Printed in the United States of America

This devotional is dedicated to my nieces and Faith Clinic Church of God in Christ. I also dedicate this book to Zion Worship Center, Going Forth Ministries, and my YWWP Sisters. Thank you for loving me!

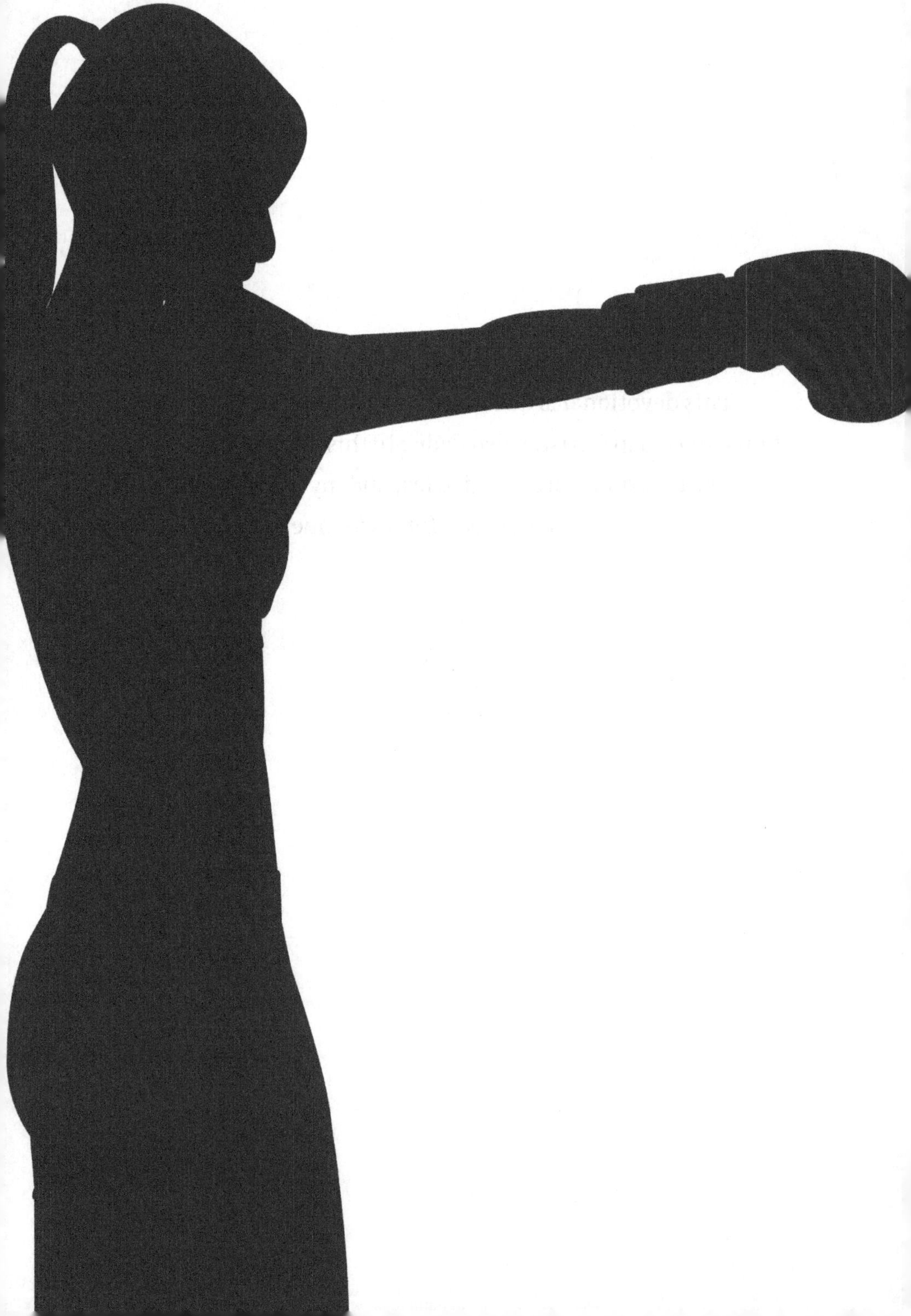

GIRL, YOU CAN WIN!

21 DAY DEVOTIONAL

TIARA MOORE

CONTENTS

Introduction   11

SECTION TITLE

Listen 16
Seeing Beyond 20
Think About This..................................... 24
Victory Has a Voice.................................. 28
From Procrastination to Pursue 32
Fearless 36
Nothing is Impossible............................... 40
Moving Past People 44
Promise Keeper 48
What's in Your Hand 52
Hidden to be Revealed.............................. 56
Getting Unstuck...................................... 60
Virtuous Does Not Mean Perfect 64
Consistency 68
May You Prosper 72
Mercy 76

GIRL YOU CAN WIN

Uproot For Your Future 80

Humility 84

Pits, Prisions, Purpose 88

Criticism 92

Winning Through Gods Love....................... 96

Promises of Victory 102

Prayer of Salvation 105

Works Cited 106

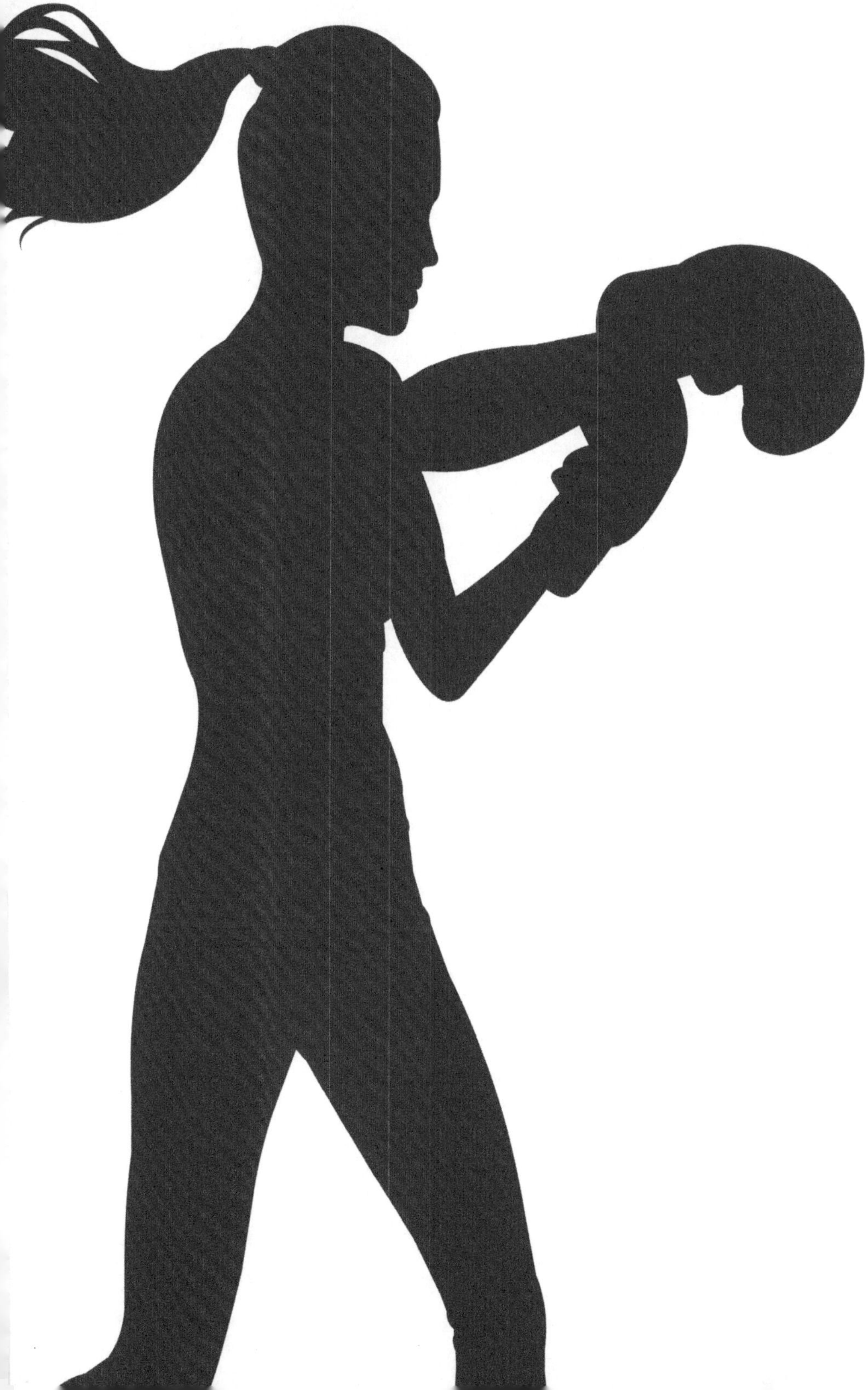

Introduction

When I first began this book, I wasn't in the actual place of winning. As of matter of fact, it was one of the hardest times of my life. I learned over time that experience is the best teacher and through trial and tribulation, life tends to give you wonderful stories you can share with others. After years of challenges and much failure, I finally felt God tugging on my heart and He whispered, "You can win." Normally when I hear His voice like this, I know it's because He has given me a personal word, and if I can hold onto that word, it becomes my next assignment. I'd always wanted to experience victory on a new level, but it was hard. Being in school full time, tackling my Master's degree, being newly engaged, and getting myself settled into ministry was difficult and time consuming. Although I had, what seemed to the naked eye, a walk of nothing but easy success, I was going home battling with internal issues. My self-esteem was steadily increasing. My goal setting skills were also becoming better, but my mind overall? Let's just say I lost several battles. One night when I climbed into my bed ready to go to sleep, I finally heard what I was waiting to hear, and that was my confirmation of victory. I've spoken with several women who all have similar stories. Some were feeling defeated by criticism and others were second guessing God's love for them. There are several other issues we will chat about later as you go on in this transformational devotional. Trust me, you will have the mindset to take whatever comes at you, not "face" on, but faith on. Remember, wherever life has found you, know that God has a bigger plan. Also understand that God is not planning your victory, but He has already destined and pre-determined, your victory. Ladies, I am not writing to you another feel good devotional. This devotional is a book of strategy tried and tested. I want to reveal to you, that if life throws lemons, you go beyond making lemonade. You have the ingredients for Godly success and the ability to walk out your God-given purpose with much strength. You are in the heart of God and were created to win. You have His breath in your nostrils, and the power of Jesus Christ rests on you perfectly at your weakest moments (2 Corinthians 12:9). Sure, we have moments where we need to be reminded that victory is a decision away, but after you remember this, I challenge you to get up and say, "Girl, you can win" regardless of the season you find yourself.

"...OVERWHELMING VICTORY IS OURS THROUGH CHRIST WHO LOVED US."

-ROMANS 8:37 NLT

DAY ONE
LISTEN

38 Now as they went on their way, Jesus[a] entered a village. And a woman named Martha welcomed him into her house. 39 And she had a sister called Mary, who sat at the Lord's feet and listened to his teaching. 40 But Martha was distracted with much serving. And she went up to him and said, "Lord, do you not care that my sister has left me to serve alone? Tell her then to help me." 41 But the Lord answered her, "Martha, Martha, you are anxious and troubled about many things, 42 but one thing is necessary.[b] Mary has chosen the good portion, which will not be taken away from her."
-Luke 10: 38-42 ESV

"**Y**ou need to relax" is a phrase I never quite understood nor wanted to understand. In my mind, if you are not busy, you are lazy. I was the woman who believed in doing everything, but still had little results. Then it happened; the Lord placed on my mind the story of Martha and Mary found in Luke chapter 10. Martha was very busy and distracted with all her serving responsibilities, and Mary was at the feet of Jesus continually listening (Luke 10:39 AMP). I wondered what this had to do with victory, and then it was very clear that in order to win, you must practice listening to the Holy Spirit. You see, while we are busy being busy, there are some emotions and even behaviors that are ignored. Jesus stated that Martha was worried, bothered, and anxious. I guarantee Martha probably had no idea she had all of these internal issues going on because at that moment, her productivity was a distraction from what would really cause her to get ahead. Mary was at the feet of Jesus and was willing to listen. How often do we find ourselves trying to find the next opportunity or doing so much for others, we neglect our self-care of hearing instructions from the Lord? Mary had listened to all she needed to hear to give her clarity and wisdom for life. Not only this, but what she retained was promised not to be taken away (Luke 10:42). Ladies, sometimes we have to sit before we move, even if it means turning off our favorite show, in order to listen. Mary demonstrates to us what really is important even when it seems like we have several other duties to tend to. Could it be that one of the struggles with winning is because we have not listened to the fact that Jesus wants us to be victorious by spending alone time with Him? He wants us to get wisdom and strategies from Him. Many of God's precious daughters have experienced burnout because we were too busy to be still. There are moments in your life where we must refuel, and that means finding time to be with Jesus before we volunteer time for the next big project. The lie that the enemy uses is that everyone is getting ahead except for us. Well, even if that is the case, I would rather sit at the feet of Jesus to get clear instructions than to consistently stay busy and be unproductive. Having a winning mentality is not about what you can do all at once, but it is about who you learn to depend upon to help you succeed in life. Before you get started with your day, be intentional and rest. I am not implying that you should sleep in daily, but I am encouraging you to rest your mind from being busy. As winning women, we must first listen to the Holy Spirit to instruct us, and while we are listening, He will renew us and strengthen us. Prioritizing His voice above our business will always produce a winning return.

PRAYER:

Father, I ask that You help me be balanced. Show me the areas of my life where I have become too busy to listen or even to hear You speaking. Restore my hunger for Your presence and fuel my faith so I trust what You say, Lord. Teach me how to be patient with myself and others as I learn to hear clearly from You, and remain productive. In the name of Jesus I pray, amen.

GIRL, YOU CAN WIN

GIRL YOU CAN WIN!
YOU NEED TO RELAX!!!

DAY TWO

SEEING BEYOND

> *35 That day when evening came, he said to his disciples, "Let us go over to the other side." 36 Leaving the crowd behind, they took him along, just as he was, in the boat. There were also other boats with him. 37 A furious squall came up, and the waves broke over the boat, so that it was nearly swamped. 38 Jesus was in the stern, sleeping on a cushion. The disciples woke him and said to him, "Teacher, don't you care if we drown?" 39 He got up, rebuked the wind and said to the waves, "Quiet! Be still!" Then the wind died down and it was completely calm.*
> *- Mark 4:35-41 NIV*

Often times, many of us face the challenges of life straight on, and although we hope and pray for the best, it seems as if God has not heard us. Some would even say it seems like He is not interested in our requests. Honestly, even the strongest believers have all faced these moments. That is what makes us human. Different seasons in our lives will cause our faith to grow, but in order for this growth to happen, we have to train our eyes to see beyond the storm. Some of these faith-growing seasons seem to be longer than we want. We have seasons when we have to accept the job that pays less just to afford our peace from difficult co-workers. Some storms are relationships that we thought would last, the marriage that fell apart, or the promotion that we never received. All storms are different but all have one thing in common; they can destroy you, but only if you are not able to see past it. Think about this; the goal that the disciples had on the boat was to get to the other side. However, they were faced with a storm that immediately triggered fear, anxiety, worry, and panic. Some of our triggers are caused because of what we are focused on or what we don't understand about storms. For instance, there are always three phases of a storm: the beginning, middle, and end. If you are not able to see the end, you will resort to having cycles, and these cycles can be vicious. If your mind is stuck on the negative, everything around you will seem bad. The bottom line is whatever you feed the most will grow. Some of us focus on the problems instead of the solutions. I am not saying this is an easy thing to do, but in order to get to the other side, whatever that may be, you have to see beyond your current situation. Jesus was on the boat during the storm, and He never left their side. As a matter of fact, scripture says He was asleep! I don't believe this was an indication that He wasn't involved, but this showed that even when we panic, Jesus already has the answer. He is not trying to conjure up a solution. He is the solution! Can you imagine how it would have been if He would have woken up and panicked right along with the disciples? Instead, He rebuked the winds, and peace and calmness followed. I am confident many of us would have run to Jesus screaming just like the disciples because all we can see is the storm devouring our lives. Not only was the storm rebuked, so was the faith of the disciples. What is revealed from within this passage is that storms not only make you stronger, but they reveal Jesus Christ. When the disciples ran to Jesus and He rebuked the storm, it obeyed His command. The disciples said within themselves with amazement, "Who is this man?" (see Luke 8:25). When you see the storms in your life, look for a revelation of who Jesus is to you in that situation. In all things see Him! This is how you train your eyes to see beyond the storm: to the most hurtful situation, He is the healer. For every unjust action done towards you, He is the vindicator. For everything that was stolen from you, He is the restorer. Be confident in knowing that you are destined to get to the other side. Challenge your eyes to see in faith and not fear. You were born to be victorious.

PRAYER:

Father, first, I ask that You forgive me for every storm I faced with complaints and frustration instead of seeking You and believing, in faith, that You have the power and authority to calm every situation in my life. I understand now that You were teaching me how to trust You in the difficult moments. Jesus, I ask that You demonstrate Your power and authority in my life, and teach me to have faith in Your plans, even when they throw mine off. I know that ultimately, You are in control of all things and I give you full access to the tough stuff I'm trying to handle on my own. I trust You, Jesus, and I thank You for walking through life with me. In the name of Jesus I pray, Amen.

DAY THREE

THINK ABOUT THIS

And now, dear brothers and sisters, one final thing. Fix your thoughts on what is true, and honorable, and right, and pure, and lovely, and admirable. Think about things that are excellent and worthy of praise.
- Philippians 4:8 NLT

Sisters, before we move forward, we must establish the thought that God has called us to be strong, confident women. We are called to be women of excellence. A woman of excellence is a woman that is praise-worthy. Proverbs chapter 31 calls this woman virtuous. When your character is in line with God's intention for His daughters, you will experience praise from both man and God. In order to walk in the calling of a woman of excellence you must manage your life by truth, not tradition. Truth is the Word of God, and tradition is whatever we have been taught that doesn't match up to God's Word. Some of these things include: women and their role in society, taking the back burner instead of leading, and feeling low self-value because we thought that thinking good thoughts of ourselves was haughty or arrogant. Being a woman is a beautiful gift and calling. We are made differently and have the strength to birth little humans. We are strong and yet gentle. We are also, often times, defeated in our minds. I've learned that doors of poor thinking habits are open during our adolescent phase of life. Maybe you made a mistake and were called out of your name for it. As a result of this negative event, the door of thinking less of yourself has been opened. For many women, being picked on and bullied, or talked about in school has resulted in them carrying these negative words and injustices for years. They've carried the insults that people slung at them without regard, and the results are the doors to overworking themselves to prove to people that you aren't a project or that you're Good enough have been opened. Your mind is the most fragile thing you have because it can break so easily. Trauma will cause you to have a jaded view of life and yourself. Some women are bound simply because their mind is in prison. Over the years we have thought about the insults, mistakes, and even the self-criticism, to the point that it has become intertwined in our identity. This is why I love what Paul says in Philippians 4:8. He says to the woman, keep your mind on the things that are good. He says this because wherever your mind is, your actions will follow and your belief system will change. You weren't created to think defeat no matter how many times you've failed. Your mind was never a place created for bondage and limitation. Instead your mind is a place to hold all of what God has said about you and about life. Romans 7:29 says it like this; With the mind we serve the law of God. Not law in the traditional sense but law in what God has said and ordained since the beginning of time. This is why you must fight so hard to think about what you're thinking about. Stinking thinking of defeat, failure, and not being good enough creates arguments that sadly, defeat several women. Some of these arguments we meditate on are toxic to our very being. Depressive thoughts become habitual. Some women feel as though they can never make it out of hard situations. Within themselves they feel burdensome; as if they are extra weight to society. These same thoughts have made women stagnant and alone, even if they're in a room full of people. Luckily these thoughts, or what scripture calls them, "arguments" don't have to have the final say. 2 Corinthians 10:5 (NIV) says; "We demolish arguments (those bad thoughts that speak to you daily) and every pretension that sets itself up against the knowledge of God, and we take captive every thought to make it obedient to Christ."

Our negative thinking must obey Christ! If God did not say what your mind is telling you, then you have the permission to take authority over it and demolish it. The word demolish means, to overwhelmingly defeat or to comprehensively refute. In other words, you take what God says as a weapon and use it toward every toxic and stinking thought. When you begin to think the right way, you see life in a whole new lens. This is why the enemy tries to usurp our thoughts. He knows if he can whisper defeat and failure, or mess with your self-esteem, you will never think highly of yourself and you will always walk with your head full of unnecessary thoughts. Maybe you've been thinking wrong for a long time, but now is the time to take control of every thought and if it doesn't align with victory, pull it down until victorious thoughts become a habit. Fix your thoughts on what is true, what is honorable, right, pure, lovely and admirable. It is not a sin to think well of yourself! God has given us the grace to help us think the right way and the authority to not allow negative thoughts to overtake you. You are called to be a woman of strength and excellence. Today I challenge you to think about what you're thinking about and if it is not victory, get it out of your mind.

PRAYER:

Father God, I ask that You would give me the mind of Christ so that I may be able to have positive and victorious thoughts. Take every stronghold that is causing me to live in negative cycles, and pull them down. I ask that You remove the residue of memories and traumatic events that take me down paths of negative thinking and release Your peace over my mind. God, I give You permission to take captive every thought that exalts itself against the knowledge of Christ. Make the mental shifts I need easy, and bring me to a peaceful state as I meditate on Your word. In the name of Jesus I pray, amen.

DAY FOUR

VICTORY HAS A VOICE

> *"Truly I say to you, whoever says to this mountain, 'Be taken up and cast into the sea,' and does not doubt in his heart, but believes that what he says is going to happen, it shall be granted him."*
> *-Mark 11:23 New American Standard*

Often times we make confessions that cause more damage than good. When we are having a bad day, we speak about how bad that day is. When we feel like we can't complete a task, we tell everyone how hard it is. This is too normal for our confessions. I have a story to tell you that may seem a little far-fetched but once I heard it, it changed the way I began to speak. To be honest, it changed the way I saw everything. I was getting ready for work and began to listen to my normal encouraging messages. My daily routine was to listen to Bishop T.D Jakes; he had become my Bishop from a distance when I needed to hear winning messages before a day's work. In his message, he made a challenging point. The Bishop said that we never read about Jesus making a table or chair, but He made a tree. As I was getting ready I was trying to figure out how that correlated with victory, and then it hit home. The point he was making is that the tree had so much to offer, but it was in the hands of the people to see and speak of its potential. On the contrary, someone could have easily said, "It's just a tree," and walked away from all it had to offer instead of saying; "This is a tree that can make paper, money, furniture, and so much more!" What we see, and what we perceive, will eventually be what we speak. Words create our future. Some of us have spoken so badly about ourselves it's no wonder our lives are the way they are currently. There are even some people who have gruesomely destroyed relationships that could have helped them because of the words that were spoken. The above scripture says something that sounds ridiculous, say to this mountain "be taken up and cast into the sea." I don't believe Jesus is telling His disciples to go to the actual mountain, but this was a message on faith and words. When you use your voice, your world can change. The problem is, most women have lost their voice. Their voice has faded into the background of life. Maybe it was because you thought your voice didn't matter. Maybe your voice was hidden behind attempts to be masculine because you thought being a lady was too soft, so you became demanding with everyone, even yourself. Perhaps you thought your voice carried no authority, so instead of speaking to life using God's word, you chose not to speak at all. I firmly believe God wants you to get your voice back. When Jesus taught His disciples how to use their faith, He taught them how to use their voice. Your voice gives faith a body. Your voice gives meaning to what you see. Your voice causes things to move. Jesus didn't use sign language for anything or anyone He encountered. He spoke. Today my sisters, I want you to get your voice back. Some women talk so lightly you can hardly hear them, and that, in most cases, is a result of them not understanding the power of their voice. You never have to shrink back again from speaking up or speaking to a situation. You may ask, "How do I use my voice?" Well for starters, if you see potential in your day, speak it! Make good use of it like the story of the fig tree, and when you see problems, speak God's word and stop it from over-taking you. Never again allow the lack of you not using your voice to be the cause of problems being persistent in your life because you can't see the potential, or because you forgot how much your voice matters. You have permission to speak to impossible situations. When your words agree with what God has said, you will surely win. Victory has a voice, all you have to do is use it.

PRAYER:

Father God, today I ask that You reactivate my voice. Give me the confidence, boldness, and faith I need to speak to impossible situations. I ask that You show me the power and authority You have given me so that I may speak and use my voice as You intended. Holy Spirit guide me and give me the wisdom to know when to speak, and when to listen for Your instructions. Heal me from the very root of why I feel as though I have no voice and give me the strength to begin to command my day with positive and victorious sayings. In Jesus' name, amen.

DAY FIVE

FROM PROCRASTINATION TO PURSUE

Do not boast about tomorrow, For you do not know what a day may bring forth.

Proverb 27:1 NIV

The thief of production is none other than procrastination. It is tragic to see how the enemy uses life to absolutely drain us and keep us tired and barren. We are tired from our 9, sometimes 12 hour work shift, which seeminlgy makes it impossible to work on your God-given purpose. Family and sometimes supporting others, drains us until we put off everything we have to do for our own lives. To be frank, we focus so much on waiting and not moving too fast that we become procrastinators. This is because some of us were told for years in church that we can't get ahead of God. We also have a mindset of supporting everyone and being at every event, so we have forgotten to support ourselves. There is a hard truth that we must understand; no matter how many financial seeds you sow, or the time you give to others, your purpose requires movement. I believe we stay so far away from doing what needs to be done concerning our own purpose and our own dreams that we create feelings of being barren. In reality we aren't barren, we just aren't moving. We've birthed a baby and named it procrastination. As women, and I can say I am guilty of this myself, many times we put off what should be completed in one day, and say to ourselves that we will get back to it. We are practicing procrastination, and to be honest, we're getting pretty good at it. I was the queen of putting off what would benefit me long term and that allowed temporary situations or responsibilities to overrule my days. This didn't change until one day I sat down and thought about a move I was preparing to take. I was mentally getting prepared to move from one state to the next, and suddenly, a light bulb came on and I saw life differently. I knew my job could replace me, I knew I couldn't change people's perceptions of whether I supported or not and I knew I had several important changes to make and important task to complete for the next chapter of my life. I believe God allows us to reevaluate our life with moments like these. We don't know what tomorrow holds but if it is in our power to do what is important at that moment, do not put it off. Instead of allowing life to drain you, manage what has to be done. Many people would be ahead if they could take back the moments when the words, "I'll get to it tomorrow" were taken out of their mindset and vocabulary. Tomorrow turns into the next day, the next day turns into the weekend, the weekend becomes a month and a month becomes a year. You've built everyone's dream but your own. You're not as barren as you think! Reorganize your commitments, break up with procrastination, and move forward.

PRAYER:

Father God, help me move forward by removing the cycle of procrastination in my life. I ask that You give me a strategy and a plan for all of the projects and tasks I have to complete. Make me formative, Lord and give me an excellent spirit. Speak to me, remind me of my assignments, and teach me how to operate with the mind of Christ so that I can multitask. I ask for the grace to get things done on time and even ahead of schedule. Shift my thoughts to give me a mindset of productivity! In Jesus' name, amen.

GIRL YOU CAN WIN!

YOUR PURPOSE REQUIRES MOVEMENT.

DAY SIX

FEARLESS

*For God hath not given us the spirit of fear;
but of power, and of love, and of a sound mind.*

2 Timothy 1:7 KJV

I've learned that fear seems to be something everyone has experienced in their life; whether it is the fear of failing, fear of losing their job, fear of being behind, or just plain old fear. The main objective of fear is to immobilize you and make you become stagnant. Sometimes fear seems rational, and in some cases God has given us these instincts to discern that something isn't right. When fear is used in that sense, it is used for its intended purpose. However, when it begins to paralyze and keep you from opportunities, that is a clear indicator that fear is trying to overcome you. Let me tell you that you can overcome fear! Fear has robbed several women of giving birth to new opportunities. This is not to say that everything you do will always work, but it also doesn't mean you do not try. There are countless inventions we use today that originally failed, but that sure didn't stop the person from trying. Never, and I mean never, stop trying; even if it isn't a success. Sometimes winning looks a lot like losing, but God uses those moments to make us and teach us. You have the God-given right to stop fear from stopping you; even if you have to attack life and opportunities afraid. I know I have. I was Ms. Timid. If fear was a super power, I definitely succeeded in having a lot of it. I was afraid to speak up for myself, afraid to make a mistake, and definitely afraid to network and build my brand and ministry. These kind of fears were a roadblock, to not only my next phase in life, but it kept me from being completely used by God. Go figure, right? That's why I am adamant on telling women everywhere that fear doesn't have to be what stops you from experiencing the best out of life. Some women live afraid. Listen, we have enough scary news being processed in hearing the news and social media articles that we cannot afford to be afraid to do what God has called us to do. Don't be afraid to venture off to see exactly what it is that you are good at doing! Successful women aren't women who always got it right, they were women who tried and learned about what fits them. Meditate on 2 Timothy 1:7; Fear is not the spirit God has given you, so, whenever fear tries to hide itself in your identity, you must identify it quickly and move forward. You are not a prisoner of fear, and you shouldn't allow it to have the authority over your life. Make the journey fun!

PRAYER:

Father God, today I ask for Your help to remove all the thoughts of torment that bring fear. During times of fear and panic, I feel out of control and even helpless. God, re-

mind me that You are in charge and that Your presence is a place of safety and protection. I ask that You give me the strength to relinquish all control to You. Anyplace there is fear in my life, remove it from the root and replace it with peace, love, and a sound mind in Jesus' name, amen.

GIRL YOU CAN WIN!

YOUR PURPOSE REQUIRES MOVEMENT.

DAY SEVEN

NOTHING IS IMPOSSIBLE

"For nothing will be impossible with God." -Luke 1:37 KJV

Have you ever stopped to ask yourself why there are moments when life can seem extremely difficult? Consider past experiences where it seemed like nothing would ever go your way. You've tried all you could and exhausted yourself and possibly others. There are moments in life where we sometimes take the steering wheel of our lives and make situations worse because of our own efforts. Let's be honest, we all have some type of God complex tucked in our DNA. Having a God complex is when you try to control every little thing. I've been there a million times. What do you do when situations seem impossible and uncontrollable? You lean totally on God. This was hard when I attempted to redefine me. I believe as women, we are evolving every single day. God created us strong; we are nurturers, mothers, naturally and spiritually, rocks of our families, mentors and coaches. We have it going on! However, when we hit hard places it is imperative that we know who to lean on. God is our hiding place (see Psalm 32:7). We must be able to give Him every single impossible situation in our life. It doesn't matter if that situation is finances, strategies, relationships, or even delayed satisfactions. With all our great qualities, we encounter impossible situations, but impossibilities are made possible with God. Don't stop at your mountain! Trust me, God doesn't want you to drain yourself when you could have simply invited Him into your impossible situations. Therefore ladies, think about all of the things in your life that have the appearance of impossible, things that you've tried to change or even people you've tried to change. Sometimes our grips are so tight, we are afraid to let God take complete control because it is so painful to give situations over that are so dear to our hearts. It is far better to place all impossibilities in the hands of God instead of burning your energy and time. God allows us to experience impossibilities so we can see His power at work. Never doubt this. Impossibilities are made possible with God.

PRAYER:

Heavenly Father, today I ask for the grace to trust You in all things. Knowing what I have to accomplish sometimes makes it difficult for me to see how You're orchestrating things behind the scenes. When I don't see You moving on my behalf, I get frustrated and try to control everything. I ask that You help me and take all matters pertaining to me

TIARA MOORE

into Your hands. You know best, and I believe in You. God give me faith for the impossible so that every mountain in my life moves when I speak to it, in the name of Jesus, amen.

GIRL YOU CAN WIN!

DON'T STOP AT YOUR MOUNTAIN!

DAY EIGHT

MOVING PAST PEOPLE

For am I now seeking the approval of man, or of God? Or am I trying to please man? If I were still trying to please man, I would not be a servant of Christ.
–Galatians 1:10 ESV

Dealing with people and what they think of me was always a personal area of weakness. I can be transparent enough to say that I've been hurt a time or two by people. See, I have a slight speech impediment. I stumble over my words and sometimes my pronunciation isn't as clear as I would like. I use to let this stop me from wanting to communicate, but instead I learned how to talk slower, louder, and more clearly. I learned how to master this flaw just enough to make it hard to spot by others, however, there are moments where it peeps out in conversations. It is mainly at work, sad to say, that because of this slight impediment people weren't so kind. My weakness was taken advantage of and some people used it against my intelligence. After noticing this, I was hurt and I questioned myself. I tried hard to prove to people that I had what it took to get the job done. This progressed into an addiction to win, which sounds good, but it was for the wrong reasons. My primary reason was to show all of them that I had it going on. My motivation was to prove a point. Maybe your impediment isn't speaking, maybe people counted you out, didn't call on you, or you felt looked over. If your heart is to win only to prove to people that you can win, you have already lost. The enemies plot against your victory is to have you moving on a hamster wheel, this wheel is to make you think that you are going somewhere when in reality you are not going anywhere at all. Paul understood this in the passage of scripture found in Galatians 1:10. He understood that he was no longer bound by man, his calling, his grace, and purpose was only to please Jesus Christ. He did not allow the opinion of man or their disqualifying thoughts hinder Him. Jesus did not allow their applause to be His motivation and He did not allow their approval to be His standard. Women who win must move past people if they are going to walk victoriously. Our ultimate goal isn't to be the smartest one in the room; it is to bring glory to Christ Jesus. One thing to keep in mind; when you free yourself from people, you are free to move in Christ and He will bring the proper attention to you, not the other

> **When you free yourself from people, you are free to move in Christ and He will bring the proper attention to you, not the other way around.**

way around. This is not to think you're better than people; this is to place your motive and perspective in a pure place. It is God who qualifies you, and sends you, and equips you, and it is Him that you please.

PRAYER:

Heavenly Father, today I ask that You heal me from every time I was offended and wounded by the words and actions of others. I have been bitter and holding onto grudges. I'm sometimes unable to think clearly or without bias. I have been defensive and rude because of the deep wounds I've received from others, but today, I ask that You heal me and forgive me. Forgive me for holding more regard for what people say and think about me than I do for Your word and Your promises for me. As You heal me Lord, removed the residue of the things that cause me to compete and esteem myself as higher, greater, or more important, than my brothers and sisters. Help me walk in love and compassion when I see the impediments of others. Bring me to a place of peace and teach me to let go of all the wrong that was done to me. Thank You, Lord for walking with me as I pursue victory, in Jesus' name, amen.

DAY NINE

PROMISE KEEPER

> 11For I know the plans I have for you," declares the LORD, "plans to prosper you and not to harm you, plans to give you hope and a future.
> - Jeremiah 29:11 NIV

Life will create questions, as it should. Some may question if God loves them enough to keep his word; which is an understandable question. What I have learned is that most questions and apprehensions we have in our hearts are based off of our experiences. Unfortunately most experiences have not always been good, and some experiences have been forgotten, so we thought, until it surfaces back at the time where we need to know that God will keep His promise. 2 Corinthians 1:20 says; For no matter how many promises God has made, they are "Yes" in Christ. And so through him the "Amen" is spoken by us to the glory of God. We have to know that God's yes isn't just for everyone else, it is for us as well. I understand it is much easier to see God keep His promises for others and fear He won't do the same for yourself, but this isn't true. If people have let us down, we place God in that same seat. If we expected God to work a miracle and it seemed like He had failed us, we would keep record. I believe God wants to correct this thinking. Numbers 23:19 says that God is not a man. This means He is not like the people who let us down, the father that walked out of some of our lives, or the people who may not have believed in us. When it comes to God working the miraculous in our life, if it doesn't happen on our time, it doesn't mean that He has forgotten, it just means that God is working on His time. Dismiss the fear that God doesn't want to perform miracles for you! The background of Jeremiah 29:11 gives us a relatable thought process that the people were thinking during that time. History says the people felt like God was not going to keep His word. They felt forgotten. God's response was a word of comfort. This comfort was to let the people know that although He knew exactly how they felt towards Him, He still had a promise that He would not take back. It is comforting to know personally that God doesn't plan to take His promise back from you. If you have ever wondered if God would take His promise back from you the answer is no. We have an immutable truth, it is not that God chooses not to lie, it is impossible for God to lie (Hebrew 6:18). The same way God chose to comfort the people in Jeremiah, He too speaks the same word to you. God knows the plans He has for you, and He plans to prosper you and never harm you. His plans are to give you hope and a future. It is not hidden from you but it has been revealed to you by his Spirit (1 Corinthians 2:10). Girl, You *can* win.

PRAYER:

God, thank You for showing me that You have not forgotten me. Sometimes when I pray I do not always feel as though You hear me. Strengthen my faith and give me the wisdom to know that You are perfecting my patience. Remind me, Heavenly Father, that You care about everything that concerns me and for that reason You have promised to never leave me nor forsake me. I declare that I have victory in every promise You made me, because Your word is truth. I ask that You continue to reveal the greatness of Your plans to me and that You will grace me to wait patiently as I reflect on Ecclesiastes 3:11. All things are done beautifully in Your timing and for this, Lord, I give You praise! In Jesus' name I pray, amen.

GIRL YOU CAN WIN!

GIRL, YOU CAN WIN!

DAY TEN

WHAT'S IN YOUR HAND?

*Then the LORD asked him (Moses),
"What is that in your hand?".....
-Exodus 4:2 NIV*

Have you ever wanted to accomplish something great but you believed that you didn't have exactly what it took to get the job done? What about the strong sense of knowing there is more to your life than what you're currently exposed to? Many times we ask God to give us more but in reality, God is asking us what is in our hands. What ideals do you have? What is in your possession right now that you can use? When you have a winning mentality, you value what is already in your hands before you search for more. In Exodus 4:2 Moses was asked what was in his hand. Now, I'm sure we know God already knew what was in his hand and how he could use it, but Moses had to see it for himself. The staff that Moses carried would be used to cause some of the greatest miracles recorded in scripture. I want to encourage you that what you have in your hands is enough. Use every disappointment, life lesson, vision, and whatever else you are holding onto and make a difference. What you have in your hands can bring freedom to others. I challenge you to never again believe that you don't have enough. When God is asking what is in your hand, He is shifting your perspective. When you are brave enough to use a small thing, God will be God-enough to do what only God can do! If what you have in your hands is nothing but mustard seed-size faith, God is able and willing to multiply it. Never allow yourself to be stuck because you don't think you have enough. Winning doesn't always start with a lot, but winning does start with you knowing you have enough. Hold out your staff Moses, and watch God divide the oceans so you can walk across on dry ground!

PRAYER:

Heavenly Father, I thank You for showing me that You can do much with little! As I prepare for the next projects and assignments in my life, I ask that You continue to be the lifter of my head. Every time I feel discouraged, send a reminder through Your word that You are the God of Ephesians 3:20. I ask for the grace to apply the works of my hands for ministry in my home, at work, in school, and in my church. Thank You for being a provider and sustainer, and Lord, thank You for consistently demonstrating supernatural multiplication in my life. Visit me with fresh creative ideas and witty inventions so I can use what's in my hands to bring You and Your kingdom glory. I ask that You anoint my hands and their works with Your consuming fire. Let everything I touch be blessed and multiply because I serve and honor You, in Jesus' name I pray, amen.

GIRL, YOU CAN WIN

GIRL YOU CAN WIN!

WHAT YOU HAVE IN YOUR HANDS CAN BRING FREEDOM TO OTHERS!

DAY ELEVEN

HIDDEN TO BE REVEALED

*4So that your giving may be in
secret. Then your Father, who sees
what is done in secret, will reward you.
Matthew 6:4 NIV*

Have you ever scrolled on social media and saw statuses that gave too much information? They shared everything with everyone. The same people that liked their status, would be the same people who wouldn't give financially to a vision. Being a woman who is dedicated to walking in victory does not require you to share every move you're making. There are conversations, prayers, and even decisions that should not be publicly announced. A wise man once said, when you mature, you become quieter, not louder. In Matthew 6:4 we see Jesus instructing the crowd that their giving should be in private. This was not to say that giving was a bad thing, but Jesus was exposing the hypocrisy in their heart. Sometimes when we overshare, we are influenced to have wrong motives in our hearts. Of this, we should be mindful. I myself was this type of woman. I thought that every good thing that happened to me was accepted by co-workers or even friends. To my surprise, people just did not care as much as I did, and it didn't make them wrong because I now understand that they are entitled to the private matters within their own lives. In addition to my surprise, I also discovered that my zeal to overshare was an attempt to feel accepted or to please those who would listen. It didn't take long to learn that I needed a safe audience to share these accomplishments with. Sisters, being a winning woman means being a woman of wisdom and discretion. This takes knowing your audience and what you can and cannot share. I encourage you to be slow to speak. What you build in secret, what you do in secret, and what you pray in secret, God will bring to the open. This is not to say that you can't say anything, but this is to say you never have to overshare to keep up with those around you or feel pressured to be relevant. You are hidden to be revealed in God's set time.

PRAYER:

Father God, Today I ask that You help me remain focused on the important matters of my day. Remind me that grace is sometimes discreet and show me how to maintain the balance of praying and saying. Your word tells me to pray about everything, but I need help with oversharing. Keep me humble and stable as I work on the projects and assignments You've graced me with. Thank You, Father for victory over my mouth, and for the wisdom and serenity to know what to do and say. Make me more like Your son, Jesus, so that I do what I see the Father do. Equip my mind for productivity and focus in the name of Jesus I pray, amen.

GIRL YOU CAN WIN!

A WISE MAN ONCE SAID, WHEN YOU MATURE, YOU BECOME QUIETER, NOT LOUDER

DAY TWELVE

GETTING UNSTUCK

> 25 Around midnight Paul and Silas were praying and singing hymns to God, and the other prisoners were listening. 26 Suddenly, there was a massive earthquake, and the prison was shaken to its foundations. All the doors immediately flew open, and the chains of every prisoner fell off!
> - Acts 16:25-26 NLT

It's a hard pill to swallow when you acknowledge that you've been stuck. Becoming stuck in a particular season in your life happens, but it does not mean that you cannot win or overcome. I've been stuck! I was stuck with certain decision I had to make. I was stuck when I changed my job and had to learn a new skill all over again. Also stuck when I got engaged and saw that I would have to relocate and start life in an unfamiliar place. I was stuck. I tried for almost a year to do everything I knew in my own strength about getting moved in the right direction. I closed and open my social media pages, I followed new diets, I hired personal trainers, only to find out nothing worked. Finally, I asked God to give me instructions that will cause me to become unstuck. The answer came and was simple; "Breathe, and get back to your secret place." I didn't know that getting unstuck took spiritual strength. Paul and Silas knew about getting unstuck. Here we see in scripture that they are in prison for preaching the good news. With normal sight all you can see is prison bars, chains, and guards making sure the prisoners never escape their current situation. If it were up to the guards they would have let Paul and Silas die behind bars. God did not stop them from being locked up, but there was a right response to their situation, and that response was praise and prayer. When Paul and Silas praised it caused an earthquake and they were suddenly loosed. Your circumstances would love for you to fall victim to being stuck and eventually forfeiting what God has created you to do. It doesn't have to end this way. Being a winning woman requires sacrifice and in most cases, that sacrifice is praise and prayer. I am convinced if Paul and Silas never would have opened their mouths to praise and pray nothing would have happened. They would have accepted defeat. What exactly was so important about their response? It demonstrated their trust in God! There are several circumstances that causes people to leave God when life gets tough but the truth is, the most successful remedy for getting unstuck is placing your trust in God wholeheartedly. If you have ever felt for a moment that you are stuck, breathe. You're not alone, but after you breathe, trust God and praise and pray your way through. As you wait, your heart will be strengthened. Winning has not left your side!

PRAYER:

Heavenly Father, today I ask that you remove any chains, barriers, and boundaries that have me in a stuck position. I chose to fall out of agreement with anything that is keeping me in an inconsistent place of prayer and praise. I choose to follow Your word and its' promise that Your Spirit sets the captives free and brings liberty. Reset my mind to receive the new balance that comes from victorious progression. Eliminate anything in the atmosphere around me that brings chaos and confusion. Lord, I renounce all cycles of stagnation in my life over my health, my finances, and my family, and I ask that You loose Your spirit to flow freely in every area of my life to bring me victory and joy. I thank you for the reminder that winning is still my present portion, in the name of Jesus I pray, amen.

GIRL YOU CAN WIN!

BREATHE, AND GET BACK TO YOUR SECRET PLACE.

DAY THIRTEEN

VIRTUOUS DOES NOT MEAN PERFECT

Favour is deceitful, and beauty is vain: but a woman that feareth the Lord, she shall be praised.
Proverb 31:30 KJV

There are moments where we get in the way as women. We are often times very hard on ourselves to be the virtuous woman we've read about in Proverbs 31. She is the type of woman that every woman aspires to become. She is admirable, a wife, mother, productive, an entrepreneur, and saved. She is everything that we want in ourselves and when we feel like she is too hard to become, we get discouraged. All of sudden, all our good is forgotten and we are back at square one. Our fight diminishes and it seems that our strength has been zapped. This is because we hold ourselves to a perfect standard that, we ourselves, cannot maintain. The truth is, we can be so hard on ourselves that we don't give ourselves enough permission to make mistakes. Being a perfectionist is one of the unhealthiest things you can ever do and be. How can we find the root? For some women, it may be the fear of being rejected because we have a history of it. For others it can be us proving ourselves to ourselves. Maybe you're trying to impress everyone around you and paint a picture that really isn't there? Or perhaps you are simply maintaining the good that everyone thinks of you already. What I've personally learned is my perfectionist habit came from trying to control uncontrollable situations. I lived to please others, even if it meant placing my heart on the line. Sure, in this generation there are several strong women that are making impactful impressions, but then there's that little girl inside that wants to stand out of the crowd. I have news for you; being virtuous does not mean you have it all together. It doesn't mean that you can color inside the lines without making any mistakes. It is not being a perfectionist. As a matter of fact, I believe the virtuous woman is a woman that learns from her mistakes. She is a woman who esteems other women, and a woman who may get it wrong, but she learns from all her mistakes. It is a woman who isn't afraid to try something new, even if she fails. She is strong and gentle, understanding and wise. The secret to being virtuous is that you become virtuous. Trial and error is necessary. Isn't that a relief? If you are hard on yourself, like I was, you can never truly walk in victory. Winning would be so hard because you think that in order to win, you don't make mistakes. Virtuous does not mean perfect. If you mess up, get up and learn from it. Use the wisdom you've learned and apply the lesson to your life. If you don't finish, start again! If you don't know the answer, look it up! Your reverence for the Lord is what makes you the woman that you are; not your beauty, your talent, nor your good deeds. Sure, it is all useful but it doesn't define you. Explore the woman that you are becoming, love her, allow her to heal from past wounds, and never find yourself getting lost in what doesn't matter.

PRAYER:

Heavenly Father, today I ask that You show me how to be a virtuous woman. Remove the negative thoughts that circle my mind, causing me to be controlling. Remind me, as often as necessary, that You are all powerful and that because You live within me, I am more than capable of being the best that I can. Be my strength and my portion. Fill my cup with Your spirit. Give me wisdom to prioritize and keep me organized. I ask that You show me how to trust You. God I ask that You keep me humble by delivering me from the need to be everything for everyone. Heal me from the negative events that make me codependent. Show me, Lord, that I am enough and that there is nothing capable of defeating me because I am full of Your Spirit, in the name of Jesus I pray, amen.

DAY FOURTEEN

CONSISTENCY

18 Then he said, "Take the arrows," and the king took them. Elisha told him, "Strike the ground." He struck it three times and stopped. 19 The man of God was angry with him and said, "You should have struck the ground five or six times; then you would have defeated Aram and completely destroyed it. But now you will defeat it only three times."
- 2 Kings 13:18-19 NIV

Consistency is something we all hear, it is also something we all desire. The pressure of finishing is more consistent than the action at times. This could be because if you don't finish right away, people will believe you may never finish. This couldn't be further from the truth! It takes persistency in every area of your life in order to be victorious. Weight loss is determined on consistency and discipline. Financial budgeting requires consistency. Successful entrepreneurship comes from consistency, and relationships require consistency. Even our prayers are a result of consistency! We cannot escape from the idea of being consistent. 2 Kings 13:18-19 paints a beautiful picture on consistency. The man of God had instructed Joash to strike his arrows, and some theologians suggest that the meaning of arrows were symbolic to prayers. Joash only struck the ground three times and gave up. The end result? He angered the man of God. Could it be that frustration is motivated by how many times we give up? Maybe he stopped because he was tired, or he may have felt fatigue along with thinking that he looked weird for continuing what he was doing. Maybe he didn't see results after his strikes, or maybe that was his way of throwing in the towel. I am sure that when you are trying there are moments you want to throw up your hands and simply give up. Your strength may get weak and you may feel fatigue, but this is not the que to throw in the towel. When you are consistent, you will see results! If you keep working your vision and keep working your goals you will see results. There is no such thing as an overnight success, but with consistency you will yield success that you are proud of because you didn't quit. Girl, you can win!

PRAYER:

God, today I ask for Your help with consistency in all I do. I seem to only be consistent in the things I like to do or in the things I know I must do. Success comes from the effort I put into the tasks and assignments before me, but Lord, I need Your help! Give me strategies and ideas that will bring me supernatural results. When I take steps to get things done, encourage me by showing me the progress I've made. Lord, make me fruitful and give me wisdom to know how to prioritize my daily schedule so that I am better able to consistently work. God, I ask for an excellent spirit so that slothfulness and laziness are never working against me. Thank you, God, for making me productive because of consistency, in the name of Jesus I pray, amen.

GIRL YOU CAN WIN!

WE CANNOT ESCAPE FROM THE IDEA OF BEING CONSISTENT.

DAY FIFTEEN

MAY YOU PROSPER

*Dear friend, I pray that you are prospering
in every way and are in good health, just as your
whole life is going well (CSB 3 John 1:2)*

Years ago I lost my job, in that process I went to a place to fill out applications. The place was filled with a mixture of people. It looked like an old high school classroom. It was the type of class where no one really paid attention because they were too busy laughing and talking the entire time. My instincts kicked in as I began walking midway through the room. I felt different and looked different from everyone in the room. It was almost like an awkward silence arose as I attempted to sit down. I began to get sick to my stomach the more I looked around, and the more I glanced at the room, the more I believed that being in that place was not a part of my purpose. I walked out and believed that God did not design me to be a woman full of comfortability by accepting life as it was handed to me. I knew there was more to me than my current situation. I understand that speaking about prosperity and even money can make several people upset. This is because we've had an incorrect view of 1 Timothy 6:10, which says, the love of money is the root of all evil. This does not mean that you cannot have money or resources, it simply means placing them in the right perspective is key. We've sat under a poor gospel for so long that it is easier to demonize success and prospering rather than teaching its priority in our life. If God calls us to glorify him, we should want to do so on our job, with our health, stewardship, and witty ideals. Prospering does glorify God; there were several Kings that God gave the permission and blessing to prosper. Idolizing prosperity is the sin and problem. This is why Paul says In Philippians 4:11, I have learned in whatsoever state I am in therewith to be content. It is not a sin to desire to prosper. I believe it was God who opened my eyes so that I could see that accepting a life for me that He didn't ordain was me giving up! That is why I walked out the way I did. It wasn't to degrade anyone in the room, however it was my epiphany that I received from heaven that the life I was preparing to settle for was not the life God wants for me. There is nothing more grievous than seeing people who are fully loaded with ideals, inventions, businesses, and ministries go through life without doing anything about it. We sit on ideals and accept what is given to us, as if it makes us humble or even worse, we are afraid to accept better. Teachings that say we should not desire to prosper are awfully misunderstood. We are not promoting worldly wealth to place before God, but we sure aren't saying, "Don't desire anything good for yourself!" That is just not the case, and God does not want you to have a poverty mindset. Contentment is good, however being comfortable and complacent is not. You don't have to settle for anything that is too low for you. God's desire is not only for you to prosper spiritually but to prosper naturally. When you prosper in your thinking, you become a significant blessing to others. You won't always have to search for resources because you will become a resource for others. Women who win are women who are brave enough to step away from comfort so that they may prosper. Will you have enough faith to believe that God does want you to prosper, or will you accept life as it is? Ultimately, the choice is yours. Don't be afraid to not only desire better, but pray for it! Ask God to help you with contentment and prospering. Ask God to help you keep Him at the forefront of your heart. Get rid of the traditional view of prosperity, because having Christ Jesus is the ultimate reward. I believe there are people that God anoints specifically in this area to advance the Kingdom! Don't ever refuse the opportunity to be blessed so that in return you may become a blessing.

PRAYER:

Heavenly Father, I ask today that You show me everywhere I am settling. If there are any plans You have for me to prosper that I am not currently following, Lord You have my permission to alter the course of my life so that my plans match Yours. I want the full portion of the promises You have made me, God. I surrender to the path and the plans You have for me to receive everything You've promised. Don't let settling be comfortable to me. God, keep me from complacency by showing me new dreams and breathing life into the dreams and visions that have not yet come into fruition. I trust You to get me to a prosperous place, Lord, and I thank You for Your grace to see it through. Give me faith to speak declarations of prosperity until I see consistent manifestation, in Jesus' name I pray, amen.

DAY SIXTEEN
MERCY

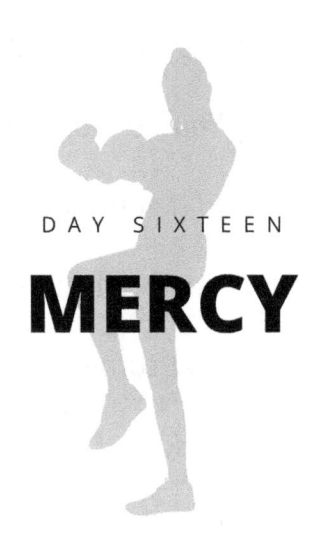

*For thou, Lord, art good, and ready to forgive;
and plenteous in mercy unto all them that call
upon thee.– Psalm 86:5 KJV*

To know God's mercy for yourself will always equip you for victory. There is nothing that can compare to the mercy of God and His goodness. God's mercy is one that is not earned and cannot be bought. You cannot earn His mercy for being good or being better than those around you. God's mercy is His gift to man and it is distributed out of His good will, and at His good pleasure. King David knew often times he was in desperate need of the mercy of God. His victory depended on God's mercy. As flawed men and women, we are dependent on God's mercy and forgiveness. The thing about the mercy of God is that it is given to those who call upon Him. I am reminded of Luke 18:38 when the blind man yelled out to Jesus to have mercy on him. Though the crowd told him to not do this, the blind man yelled out again have mercy on me.

Jesus stood still, commanded the man to be brought near Him, and asked the man what he wanted Him to do for him. Mercy was given when the man demonstrated his belief in who Jesus was by calling out to Him for mercy. The man's sight was restored. We are all in need of the mercy of God. Everything around us may act like the opposing voice that attempted to quiet the blind man in Luke (See Luke 18). We must go beyond what is pulling us back and ask God for His Mercy. If it wasn't for the mercy of God we would all be disqualified from prospering. Several women have disqualified themselves from God's best simply because they had not known that His mercy was available to them. Women who are determined to win are women who can confess that if it had not been for the mercy of God they would not be where they are. His mercy cleanses you from your past mistakes, and even the parts of you that are not deserving of moving forward. His mercy holds back what we truly deserve. You never have to allow people or your past to tell you that you don't deserve to walk victoriously. You are a woman who can win because God's mercy, grace, and forgiveness accompanies you and qualifies you daily when you call upon Him. Whenever you feel like you're bound and can't win, call upon God's mercy. It is available to you and given to you with good pleasure.

PRAYER:

Heavenly Father, thank You for Your mercy that accompanies me in my life. Forgive me for the times I forgot about Your mercy. I ask for Your grace and mercy to walk in victory.

Bring to my remembrance the love I have from You through Christ Jesus. Renew my mind to know that I can be a woman who can win life's battles as I depend on You every step of the way. Teach me to be merciful to others, because in doing so, I know You will show mercy to me. Father God, I know You hear me when I call upon you, and I thank You for always stopping and giving me exactly what I need, in the name of Jesus I pray, amen.

GIRL YOU CAN WIN!

YOU ARE A WOMAN WHO CAN WIN BECAUSE GOD'S MERCY

DAY SEVENTEEN

UPROOT FOR YOUR FUTURE

31 Get rid of all bitterness, rage and anger, brawling and slander, along with every form of malice. 32 Be kind and compassionate to one another, forgiving each other, just as in Christ God forgave you.
-Ephesians 4:31-32 NIV

As women we must be very attentive to our hearts. As incubators and nurturers it is possible that we can nurture our problems, unhealthy relationships, and also bitterness. These emotions love hiding in our hearts and manifesting during times where we need to step out and do something courageous. We've hidden negative emotions in the way we cope. Without dealing with the toxic roots of bitterness, un-forgiveness, or depression, which is anger unexpressed, we can be our biggest hindrance. It is not okay to allow negative emotions to rest in your heart, even if it is in the "name" of being a strong woman. It is okay to cry. It is okay to let it all out, Psalm 34:18-19 tells us the LORD is close to the brokenhearted and saves those who are crushed in spirit. The scriptures goes on to say; The righteous person may have many troubles, but the LORD delivers him from them all. Whenever we speak of uprooting it is something we hardly ever have to do alone. God is with us to help us uproot, but it takes us being honest. The emotions that are revealed are because God wants to heal them. It doesn't make you any less of a woman when you self-evaluate and find the "not so good" emotions. It makes you human. Look at Psalm 73:26; "My flesh and my heart may fail, but God is the strength of my heart and my portion forever." That forever is something you can count on. Most women would say; "well, I'm not dealing with any heart issues." Be careful not to be too confident in this area. 2 Corinthians 10:12 "If you think you are standing strong, be careful not to fall." If you're not dealing with something today I applaud you, but if you deal with anything now, this will be useful and for the future, it will be helpful. Now concerning the heart, Jeremiah 17:9 says; "The heart is deceitful above all things, and it is exceedingly corrupt: who can know it but God." I literally cringe when I hear women say something completely out of line and turn around and say; "God knows my heart!" After today, let's agree to never say this again. The heart is tricky, and I ask God every day to forgive and heal what I am not aware of. Negative emotions, unforgiveness and hurt can be hidden in several ways. For myself, I hid. I hid in the gym for hours, I hid in church activities, I hid in outbursts of crying or even dealing with people in picturing the face of others who may have hurt me (I know, it sounds ridiculous but it is true!). I hid the issues of my heart. It took a while for me to understand that this is not the loving will of the Father for your life. My guard was lifted up once someone did something similar to those that may have offended me, and in return, they were mistreated or handled at a distance because of my apprehension that rooted from my heart that carried bitterness. Maybe you are not a woman who carries bitterness, but maybe you're a woman who finds it hard to forgive. Perhaps you are a woman who has carried hurt in her heart and wondered why it seemed like you weren't getting ahead. God wants to heal you, He wants you to surrender all emotions that are toxic to your victory. Don't feel bad for having these emotions. They are normal, however, do something different when these emotions arise; pay attention to how you respond to situations. If you find yourself responding incorrectly, do not condemn yourself, but cast those cares upon the Lord who so desperately cares for you and he will never let you be shaken (Psalm 55:22).

PRAYER:

Lord, today I ask that You help me uproot everything that I have not been able to heal from. All the things from my past that weigh me down and cause me to respond to people in bitterness and unforgiveness, I ask that You would remove them from me. Cleanse me spiritually and restore the fragmented pieces of my soul so I may move forward in the purpose and plans You have for me. God, heal me from the offenses I've suffered and bring a fresh wave of peace to my mind. Flood my spirit with faith! Not only do You heal, but

Lord, You make whole! I ask for wholeness, in the name of Jesus I pray, amen.

DAY EIGHTEEN
HUMILITY

*For even the Son of Man came not to be served but
to serve others and to give his life as a ransom for many."
–Matthew 20:28 NLT*

Jesus came not to be served, but to serve. This is food for thought that the ruler of everything did not come to be served, but to be a servant. Walking and imitating Christ gives us the key to not only success and victory, but the keys to life. If you want to be a woman who wins, it is wise to be strong and humble. Many women are not winning simply because we have become too self-dependent, arrogant, or prideful. These are the ingredients of failure; even when it looks like you may be winning. True success is not about what we can gain, it is about what we can give. Jesus did not only demonstrate His humility with servanthood, but also with His ability to stand against crucial mistreatment. He was so confident in Himself and His purpose, that He did not have to prove Himself to anyone. I want to share with the winning woman that your humility will always open doors. What you do for others will always place you in the perfect posture of victory. Nothing can stop the humble. 1Peter 5:5-6 says that; "God resists the proud, but gives grace to the humble. Therefore humble yourselves under the mighty hand of God, that He may exalt you in due time." This mentality will cause you to always walk victoriously. Humility makes you courageous, and while the world is focused on serving only themselves, victorious women have found the treasure in serving others. Jesus lived a life of servitude. He exemplified true humility and obedience, and because of this He was glorified. Humility comes before honor. I challenge you to be women that are bold enough to be humble!

PRAYER:

Heavenly Father, today I ask You to show me the true meaning of humility. Through Your word, I see how Jesus served all. I ask, God, that You show me how to be a servant to my family and others. Expose every prideful and self-centered area of my life and lead me down a humble path. Only You can change my nature and behavior to mirror Christ, and I thank You that grace and mercy have allowed me to get to the place where I am now. I believe the more I serve others, the more You will open doors for me. Teach me Your ways God, and remove egotistical, vain, and self-serving behaviors, in the name of Jesus I pray, amen.

GIRL YOU CAN WIN!

TRUE SUCCESS IS NOT ABOUT WHAT WE CAN GAIN, IT IS ABOUT WHAT WE CAN GIVE.

DAY NINETEEN

PITS, PRISON, PURPOSE

20 Joseph's master took him and put him in prison, the place where the king's prisoners were confined. But while Joseph was there in the prison, 21 the Lord was with him; he showed him kindness and granted him favor in the eyes of the prison warden. 22 So the warden put Joseph in charge of all those held in the prison, and he was made responsible for all that was done there. 23 The warden paid no attention to anything under Joseph's care, because the Lord was with Joseph and gave him success in whatever he did.
Genesis 39:20-23 NIV -2 Timothy 1:7 KJV

Part of growing into yourself and becoming a woman who wins is using what seems to be a negative as a positive. The negative is what I like to call "pits and prisons." Of course it sounds simple, but when I listen to women who may need some form of counsel what I hear repetitively is that the woman may not be used to her pit and prison season. That is partly because pits and prisons are not likely the place where the average person may run. They're lonely, outcasts, and there is a lack of every resource imaginable. Pits and prisons are not a happy place, however they are in our lives to catapult us into destiny. For one, Joseph was tossed in his pit by his brothers (Genesis 37:24). His brothers threw him into his pit out of jealousy and they refused to say one kind word to him. Joseph was favored and loved by his father so much that his father made him a special coat. His Father's love placed a target on him. I am confident that many of us women may feel like we have a target on us. Everywhere we turn it seems like we keep running into the same betrayal or dry season. Like Joseph, there are some women that may feel like the black sheep in their family or close friends. These close relatives and friends are the ones who, like Joseph's brothers, envy you because they may notice the favor on your life. The next P is prison. It may feel like you are tossed into a prison; completely locked up before you actually reach the place of purpose. You've learned how to move past people, and you understand that all along you were dealing with jealousy and the harshness of others hearts. You thought the season of being in that place was over, but it escalates to feeling like captivity. It seems like right before you receive your breakthrough, there is another level of feeling hurt, insecurities, betrayal, and doubts that resurfaces. When this happened to me, I would always think that I was headed to my next place. I remember the times I was completely lied on, but all I needed was to hold my peace and God handled the rest. I knew I would receive favor from whom I needed it. I find it interesting that this was how Joseph's life was. He was lied on and tossed in the prison, however the scripture says in Genesis 39; "The Lord was with him and showed him faithful love." However my favorite verse ends with; "The Lord was with him and caused everything he did to succeed" (see Genesis 39:19-23). Finally Joseph's moment had come. The pit and prison made sense. Joseph's faithfulness to God, through all the mistreatment, allowed his gifts to make room for him. He was processed within his character to go to the Palace. This teaches us the 3 P's he experienced: pit, prison and palace, are all necessary. If we keep that type of forward thinking you will easily adapt a winning mentality. Normally when you are in a pit, God is doing something special for you. He is removing the people who would normally block you. This work and character development is on your mind, your tenacity, and your perception. The strength you gain in the pit is incomparable. It is the key that unlocks real humility. It teaches you how to serve; especially when there is a purpose that is outside of your own. Before Joseph could be in the palace and placed in his rightful position, he suffered. The pit always appears as a place of suffering, but the pit is a place of making and molding. When we are placed in those hard places it is strategically made to build you, and to add to your character, and to try your faithfulness. It is like a fine fire set out to burn away the dross and everything attached to you that is not beneficial to you or to where you're going. Hard places are not always bad, although it may be physiologically tough. In Joseph's case, it was the key to his favor and exposure. His journey was perfectly planned by God. After Joseph survived his hard places, he brought tremendous glory to God. This should be our aim. When you are going through you're never alone, but when you come out, you will be used as the influencer and strong woman that you are.

PRAYER:

Heavenly Father, today I ask for the strength to recognize and face my pit and prison seasons. These are two plac-

es I do not want to be in, however, I now understand they are necessary. I ask that You teach me all I need to know to successfully carry out the great assignments on my life. God strengthen and encourage me in the low place. Be the lifter of my head and shield me from distractions while I am being molded and processed. I ask that You teach me to have the character of Jesus. Walk with me, Lord, and give me favor that causes everything I do to succeed. I ask for wisdom during my low season, and for the Holy Spirit to visit me and be my constant guide. Thank You, God for teaching me humility before exaltation, in the name of Jesus I pray, amen.

DAY TWENTY

CRITICISM

At last the wall was completed to half its height around the entire city, for the people had worked with enthusiasm.
-Nehemiah 4:6 NLT

One thing about criticism is that it is never comfortable. Criticism is something you have to learn and work through. Although criticism may hurt, it is something that we can use in our arsenal. If you are courageous enough to move forward into destiny, then you must be courageous enough to accept hard words and even the thoughts from others. The first thing you'll learn is their opinions, though there may be many, do not reflect the winning woman you are. For instance, I can recall a moment in my life when I was criticized about a certain small mistake I made on my job. I was new and so focused on planning a wedding and moving away, that I made a human error. I could hear the whispers and felt the temperature of the room change everytime

I would walk in. The sad thing is, it wasn't from everyone, it was only from the older woman who spoke rudely to everyone. To be honest, I felt inadequate. I knew that I was impressively wise and could articulate extremely well when I worked my strengths, but to them, I was the new girl who knew nothing. I fought to keep my mouth shut from bragging about all my accomplishments. I fought even harder to encourage myself by saying things like; "Come on Tee! You're doing a great job!" That is because their criticism, or my colleague's critique, made me second guess my actual strengths. Let's look at Nehemiah 4:1-3. "Sanballat heard that Nehemiah was rebuilding the wall, he became angry and was greatly incensed. He ridiculed the Jews, 2and in the presence of his associates and the army of Samaria, he said, "What are those feeble Jews doing? Will they restore their wall? Will they offer sacrifices? Will they finish in a day? Can they bring the stones back to life from those heaps of rubble-burned as they are?" 3Tobiah the Ammonite, who was at his side, said, "What they are building-even a fox climbing up on it would break down their wall of stones!" As you can see, that was a pretty harsh critique. Moment of transparency: I was never a fan of criticism until I learned how to use it. Any woman or leader who wants to succeed will be measured. The measurement is because you attract attention. When you walk in the room, you are noticed and not invisible. There are nuggets in criticism that you can take away and improve yourself with, and then there is criticism that you have to disregard in its totality. The old terminology is eating the meat and spitting out the bones. Every person under the sun will be criticized. If you decide to marry a certain person, you're criticized. If you choose a new career path, start a business, or choose how to raise your family, you are criticized. Although you are criticized, do not quit!

People who quit because of criticism miss out on an opportunity to perfect whatever it is they are aiming towards. Criticism is not a time to shrink back. Keep building in the midst of criticism. More than likely when you are criticized, the opinions are the opposite of your true ability. As long as you plan to do more than what people are accustomed to, you will be criticized. Never allow your distinctiveness to be criticized by a limited person with minimum exposure to who you are. People will talk because of how they think, you cannot control this so never allow it to control you.

PRAYER:

Heavenly Father, today I ask for Your help concerning criticism and the negative words that are being spoken against me. Help me to see You in all things concerning my purpose. If there are areas of my life that need work, show me how to use the criticism as fuel. Father I also ask that You heal me from the offensive words that come from the opinions of others. Show me how to set my face like flint, and give me the tools I need to be empowered by the affirmations and validations of Your word. Holy Spirit, I ask that You comfort me as I do all my work as unto the Lord. Thank You for teaching me to have an excellent spirit and for molding my character to mirror Christ. I am victorious because of Your example! In the name of Jesus I pray, amen.

DAY TWENTY ONE

WINNING THROUGH GOD'S LOVE

By Janisha Bessiake

*At last the wall was completed to half its height around
the entire city, for the people had worked with enthusiasm.
Nehemiah 4:6 NLT*

I remember when people would say " Don't you know that God loves you?" I would respond back and say, "yes." Or when I would take the time to read the word of God myself, it was repetitive scriptures that would make it clear that I am/we are loved by God. However if I can be honest, I didn't really believe that God could love me the way the bible explains it. Just like me, others can't really wrap their heads around being loved by God and receiving God's love. As my relationship matured with God, here is one of the several things I began to learn. Many of us often see God through the lens of our parents. We think that God's love is like the love we were shown inside our home, or how we were loved growing up. This is mainly because the home we grew up in defined everything for us. The major thing that home defines is what love is, and what love looks like. Many different people have experienced different things. Let me give you an example. Sarah's father wasn't emotionally present. The clinical term for that is called emotional abandonment. As an adult Sarah has always cleaved to any man who says nice things to her, even if they are lying. James' mother didn't show grace growing up. He didn't have room to fail unless getting punished for making mistakes. As an adult, James thinks that people, including himself, should be perfect. Let's say they both give their life to Christ and they enter into Christianity believing that God loves as their parents love. In their/our immaturity, we already expect God to love us as our parents do. The Good and the Bad. They begin to assume that God is this way, but what they soon find out is that He's not the way they thought. Just like James and Sarah, we've been seeing God through the lens of our natural father's and mother's love. We see God through our struggles and pain. We must be able to see God through the lens of what He says love is. Here is how God describes his love:

> **Many of us often see God through the lens of our parents.**

Love is patient, love is kind. It does not envy, it does not boast, it is not proud. It does not dishonor others, it is not self-seeking, it is not easily angered, it keeps no record of wrongs. Love does not delight in evil but rejoices with the truth, It always protects, always trusts, always hopes, always perseveres. -1 Corinthians 13: 4-7 NIV

*Whoever does not love does not know God, because God is love.
-1 John 4:8 NIV*

There is no fear in love. But perfect love drives out fear because fear has to do with punishment. The one who fears is not made perfect in love. -1 John 4:18 NIV

*The LORD appeared to us in the past saying: " I have loved you with an everlasting love; I have drawn you with unfailing kindness.
-Jeremiah 31:3 NIV*

    These scriptures are just four out of many that tell us about being loved by God. Sarah begins to understand that she needed to unlearn how being loved looked, and how she defined it based on how it was taught to her. James needed to do the same thing, and, so do we. We need to unlearn what love is, and how love looks to us. What that looks like is acknowledging and becoming aware of how we have defined and viewed love for all these years. For Sarah, she had to acknowledge that God is intimate, and He is present all the time in every way. She had to believe God for who He is instead of expecting God to love her based on the area where her natural father lacked. James also had to acknowledge that God is a God of grace and patience. He realized that God is not going to punish him for making mistakes. With God, he is safe to fail so that he can develop, learn, and grow.

    The scriptures are not just telling us what love is, but they're communicating to us that God embodies love. He is love. However love is defined and described, that's who He is. Sarah and James will begin to heal from the areas where they did lack love. As they begin to fill those empty spaces with the love of God and the Word of God, their minds begin to transform. Their definition of love, and being willing to receive a new kind of love, changed. They were able to receive God's love in the purity of what it is. Nothing added to it. I want the same for you! I want you to be perfectly loved by God. God's love is perfect and unconditional. God's love is eternal and it's not based on conditions. He loves us when we are right, and He loves us when we are wrong. If God's love is perfect and we are made in the image of God, then we are a perfect manifestation of the love of God. My prayer recently has been, "God I just want to be loved well by You." Understanding God for who He said He is, believing it, and receiving it, has made me secure. It has made me realize that no matter what, I'm loved, and not just regularly loved, I'm loved by a perfect God. He has the ability to love us perfectly. Girl, you better get you some! It's a journey and it takes work. However, I hope and pray that you begin your work, and begin your journey of being LOVED WELL BY GOD. Girl, you can not only win, but you have already won!

PRAYER:

Heavenly Father, today I ask for Your help concerning criticism and the negative words that are being spoken against me. Help me to see You in all things concerning my purpose. If there are areas of my life that need work, show me how to use the criticism as fuel. Father I also ask that You heal me from the offensive words that come from the opinions of others. Show me how to set my face like flint, and give me the tools I need to be empowered by the affirmations and validations of Your word. Holy Spirit, I ask that You comfort me as I do all my work as unto the Lord. Thank You for teaching me to have an excellent spirit and for molding my character to mirror Christ. I am victorious because of Your example! In the name of Jesus I pray, amen.

GIRL YOU CAN WIN!

GIRL, YOU ALREADY WON!

GIRL YOU CAN WIN

Promises of Victory

1 Corinthian. 15:57 KJV "But thanks be to God, which giveth us the victory through our LORD Jesus Christ."

Psalms. 118:6 KJV "The LORD is on my side; I will not fear: what can man do unto me?"

Psalms. 37:39-40 NKJV "But the salvation of the righteous is of the LORD: He is their strength in the time of trouble. And the LORD shall help them, and deliver them: He shall deliver them from the wicked, and save them, because they trust in Him."

Romans. 8:31 NIV "What shall we then say to these things? If God be for us, who can be against us?"

Psalms. 100:5 KJV "For the LORD is Good; His mercy is everlasting; and His Truth endureth to all generations."

1 John 5:15 NIV "And if we know that He hear us, whatsoever we ask, we know that we have the petitions that we desired of Him."

Nahum. 1:7 KJV "The LORD is Good, a Strong Hold in the day of trouble; and He knoweth them that trust in Him."

Hebrews. 4:16 KJV "Let us therefore come boldly unto the throne of grace, that we may obtain mercy, and find grace to help in time of need."

Psalms. 63:7 KJV "Because Thou hast been my Help, therefore in the shadow of Thy wings will I rejoice."

Psalms. 33:20 NIV "Our soul waiteth for the LORD: He is our Help and our Shield

Isaiah. 41:13 KJV "For I the LORD thy God will hold thy right hand, saying unto thee, Fear not; I will help thee."

Deuteronomy 20:4 KJV - For the LORD your God [is] he that goeth with you, to fight for you against your enemies, to save you.
Philippians 4:13 KJV- I can do all things through Christ which strengtheneth me.

John 16:33 KJV - These things I have spoken unto you, that in me ye might have peace. In the world ye shall have tribulation: but be of good cheer; I have overcome the world.

Psalms 108:13 KJV - Through God we shall do valiantly: for he [it is that] shall tread down our enemies.

1 Corinthians 10:13 KJV - There hath no temptation taken you but such as is common to man: but God [is] faithful, who will not suffer you to be tempted above that ye are able; but will with the temptation also make a way to escape, that ye may be able to bear [it].

2 Corinthians 12:9-10 KJV - And he said unto me, My grace is sufficient for thee: for my strength is made perfect in weakness. Most gladly therefore will I rather glory in my infirmities, that the power of Christ may rest upon me.

1 Corinthians 15:57 KJV - But thanks [be] to God, which giveth us the victory through our Lord Jesus Christ.

Ephesians 6:10 KJV - Finally, my brethren, be strong in the Lord, and in the power of his might.

Jeremiah 29:11 NLT For I know the plans I have for you," says the Lord. "They are plans for good and not for disaster, to give you a future and a hope.

Philippians 4:19 NLT And this same God who takes care of me will supply all your needs from his glorious riches, which have been given to us in Christ Jesus.

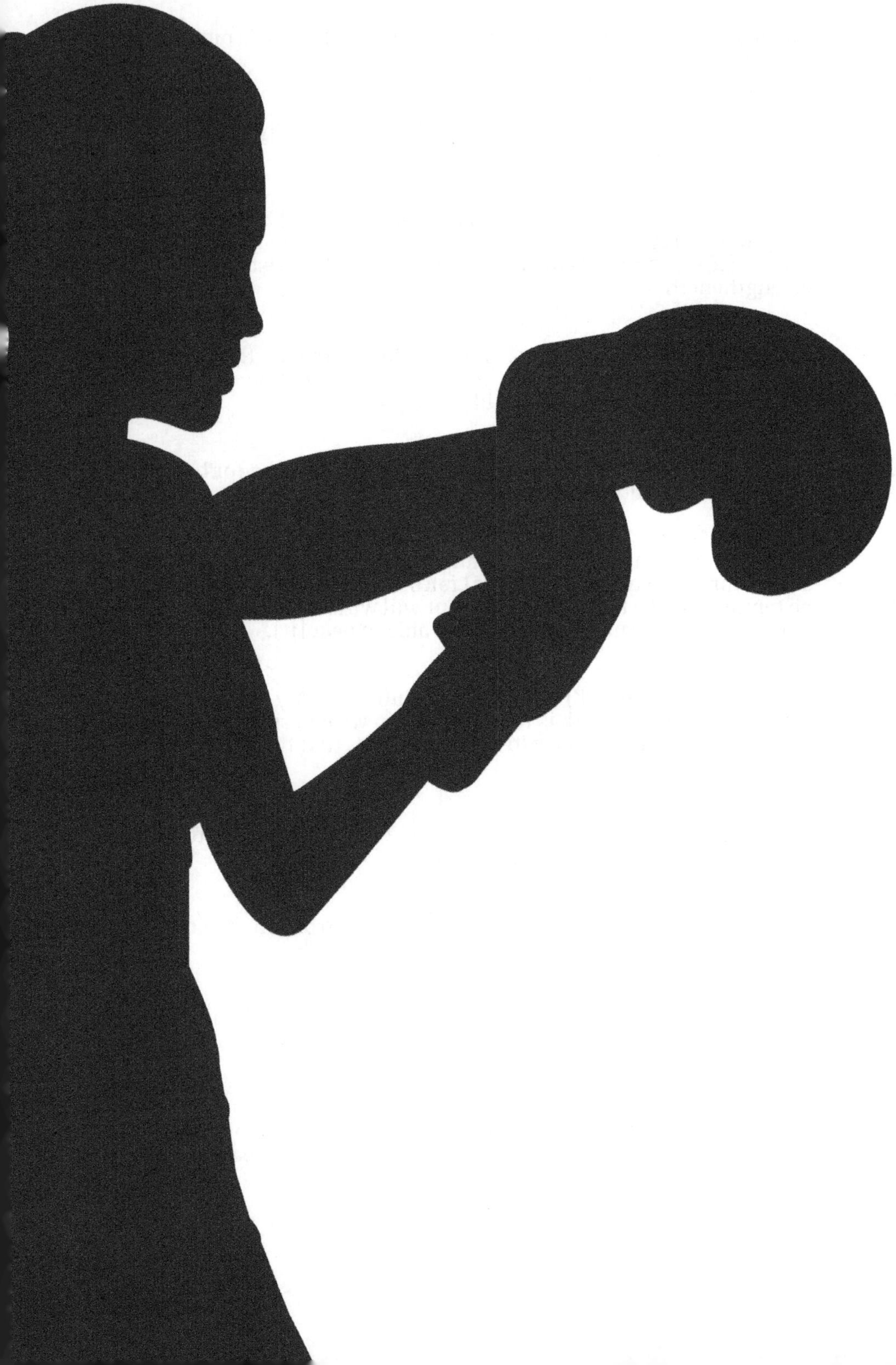

GIRL YOU CAN WIN

Prayer of Salvation

Lord Jesus,

I come to You in prayer as a sinner, asking Your forgiveness. I believe in my heart and confess with my mouth that You are the Son of God. I believe in my heart that You came, and lived a sinless life. I believe that You took my sin upon You and died on my behalf.

I declare You are Lord of my life, and accept You as my savior! Thank You for Your forgiveness. By the blood of Jesus, I declare I am saved!

As I live each day, continue to reveal Your love to me by Your Holy Spirit. I am a new creation!

In Jesus' name,
Amen!

GIRL YOU CAN WIN
Work Cited

Holy Bible: English Standard Version. 2001. Wheaton, IL: Crossway Bibles of Good News Publishers.

Holy Bible: Holman Christian Standard Version. 2009. Nashville: Holman Bible Publishers.

Holy Bible: King James Version. 1999. New York, NY: American Bible Society.

Holy Bible: New American Standard Bible. 1995. LaHabra, CA: The Lockman Foundation.

Holy Bible: New International Version. 1984. Grand Rapids, MI: Zondervan Publishers.

Holy Bible: New King James Version. 1982. Nashville, TN: Thomas Nelson Publishing.

Holy Bible: New Living Translation. 2015. Carol Stream, IL: Tyndale House Publishers.

Made in the USA
Middletown, DE
21 August 2024